THE THINK & GROW RICH ROADMAP

THE THINK AND GROW RICH ROADMAP.

Copyright © 2025 by Bluestone Books.

All rights reserved.

Any unauthorized duplication in whole or in part or dissemination of this edition by any means (including but not limited to photocopying, electronic devices, digital versions, and the internet) will be prosecuted to the fullest extent of the law.

www.bluestonebooks.co

ISBN: 978-1-965636-03-9 (paperback)

Design by Joanna Williams
Edited by Jennifer Leight

Illustrations used under license from Shutterstock

Printed in the United States of America
First Edition: 2025

10 9 8 7 6 5 4 3 2 1

THE THINK & GROW RICH ROADMAP

PRACTICAL STEPS AND TRANSFORMATIONAL EXERCISES FOR A PERSONAL BLUEPRINT TO WEALTH

Adapted from the Classic
Think and Grow Rich by Napoleon Hill

BLUESTONE BOOKS

CONTENTS

Introduction 7

1 DESIRE 9
The first step toward riches: Spark a burning desire to be successful.

2 FAITH 23
Develop unwavering belief in your ability to achieve your goals.

3 AUTO-SUGGESTION 35
Influence your subconscious mind with positive self-talk.

4 SPECIALIZED KNOWLEDGE 45
Focus on what you need relevant to your goals.

5 IMAGINATION 55
Unlock ideas and plans to achieve success through visionary thinking.

6 ORGANIZED PLANNING 67
Create a concrete plan to achieve your goals and take actionable steps.

7 DECISION 77
Cultivate the ability to make firm decisions and avoid procrastination.

8 PERSISTENCE **89**
Push forward despite challenges and setbacks.

9 THE MASTER MIND **101**
Surround yourself with people who support and contribute to your success.

10 THE MYSTERY OF SEX TRANSMUTATION **113**
Channel powerful energy into creative and productive outlets.

11 THE SUBCONSCIOUS MIND **125**
Master your subconscious mind to align with your goals.

12 THE BRAIN **137**
Recognize your mind as both transmitter and receiver to attract opportunities.

13 THE SIXTH SENSE **147**
Tap into your intuition and develop a deeper understanding of life and success.

Your Custom Roadmap 159

Daily Practice Trackers 160

"Riches begin in the form of thought!"

INTRODUCTION

So much feels uncertain these days. Markets rise and fall overnight. Jobs evolve, disappear, and reappear in forms we never imagined. It's easy to feel like the path to success is out of your hands. But one thing is always within your control: your mind.

Napoleon Hill knew this better than anyone. Long before podcasts, life coaches, or social media influencers, he dedicated twenty-five years of his life to studying the world's most successful people—at the direct request of Andrew Carnegie. The result was *Think and Grow Rich*, first published in 1937 and still one of the best-selling personal development books of all time.

Why does a nearly century-old book continue to resonate? Because it's not just about getting rich. It's about discovering how your thoughts, beliefs, and habits shape your reality—financially, yes, but also mentally, emotionally, and spiritually. Hill didn't just share feel-good ideas; he laid out a practical, step-by-step formula based on real lives and proven patterns. From Edison and Ford to ordinary people achieving extraordinary results, the message is clear: You become what you think about most. This workbook is your guide to putting that truth into action.

Over the next ninety days, you'll walk through Hill's thirteen timeless principles—one per week—with a fresh focus each day. Every chapter introduces a core concept from *Think and Grow Rich*, then invites you to explore it deeply through writing, reflection, and practical exercises. You'll build clarity, develop new habits, and discover how to align your thoughts and actions with your deepest goals.

It's important to note that this is a companion, not a substitute. This workbook is designed to be used alongside—or just after you've read—*Think and Grow Rich*. Hill's original text contains the full philosophy, historical examples, and foundational ideas behind each principle. This workbook simply helps you slow down, personalize, and apply what you learn.

Whether you're aiming to grow a business, switch careers, build confidence, or unlock financial freedom, Hill's tools still work—because they're rooted in how the human mind works. And your mind is the one thing in this unpredictable world that you can shape with intention.

So let's begin. Open your mind, commit to the process, and take the first step toward mastering the one thing that has the power to transform everything: your thinking. You don't have to control the economy. You just have to control what's possible through you.

1

DESIRE

**The first step toward riches:
Spark a burning desire to be successful.**

"The starting point of all achievement is desire. Keep this constantly in mind. Weak desire brings weak results, just as a small fire makes a small amount of heat."

Edwin C. Barnes had a burning desire: to be in business with (not *for*) the great inventor Thomas A. Edison. It took more than five years from the first time Barnes hopped off a freight train in New Jersey and met Edison face-to-face for this to become a reality. But the burning desire—not a wish, not a hope—was birthed and committed to much earlier than that.

Just how great does your desire need to be to make it a reality? You must be willing to go past the point of no return, according to Hill:

"A long while ago, a great warrior faced a situation which made it necessary for him to make a decision which insured his success on the battlefield. He was about to send his armies against a powerful foe, whose men outnumbered his own. He loaded his soldiers into boats, sailed to the enemy's country, unloaded soldiers and equipment, then gave the order to burn the ships that had carried them. Addressing his men before the first battle, he said, 'You see the boats going up in smoke. That means that we cannot leave these shores alive unless we win! We now have no choice—*we win—or we perish!*' They won.

"Every person who wins in any undertaking must be willing to burn his ships and cut all sources of retreat. Only by so doing can one be sure of maintaining that state of mind known as a burning desire to win, essential to success. . . .

"*Wishing* will not bring riches. But *desiring* riches with a state of mind that becomes an obsession, then planning definite ways and means to acquire riches, and backing those plans with persistence which *does not recognize failure*, will bring riches."

In this chapter, you will clearly define your desire, fuel it for success, and burn anything that could hold you back. The steps are based on wisdom Hill gathered from history's success stories and "were carefully scrutinized by . . . Thomas A. Edison, who placed his stamp of approval upon them as being, not only the steps essential for the accumulation of money, but necessary for the attainment of *any definite goal.*

"The steps call for no 'hard labor.' They call for no sacrifice. They do not require one to become ridiculous, or credulous. To apply them calls for no great amount of education. But the successful application of these . . . steps does call for sufficient *imagination* to enable one to see, and to understand, that accumulation of money cannot be left to chance, good fortune, and luck." Get ready to declare and claim your desire.

EXERCISE 1
The Desire Declaration

Create a powerful written statement to fix your mind on your goal.

Write a short but deep declaration of your burning desire. It should be specific, time-bound, and written in the present tense as though it were already achieved. Example: "I am earning [exact amount] annually by [date]."

_____
_____
_____
_____
_____
_____
_____
_____
_____

> *"There is a difference between wishing for a thing and being ready to receive it. No one is ready for a thing, until he believes he can acquire it. The state of mind must be belief, not mere hope or wish."*

Thinking about your desire, ask yourself, "Why do I want this?" Write down your answer. Repeat this process four more times, each time digging deeper into the reasons behind your desire.

1 _____

2 _____

3 _____

4 _____

5 _____

EXERCISE 2
Measuring Your Intention

Assess and stoke the intensity of your desire.

On a scale of 1–10, rate your desire to achieve your goal.

What words describe the intensity of your desire now? Write them in the left column. What words would drive that desire to where it needs to be? Add them to Hill's words in the right column.

	definite
	dominating
	pulsating
	transcendent

What are you willing to do to get to a 10 on the desire scale?

"There is no such reality as 'something for nothing.'"

EXERCISE 3
A Clear Path for Action

Get rid of limiting thoughts and the possibility of failure.

"[Barnes] did not say to himself, 'I will try to induce Edison to give me a job of some sort.'

"He did not say, 'I will work there for a few months, and if I get no encouragement, I will quit and get a job somewhere else.'

"He did not say, 'I will keep my eyes open for another opportunity, in case I fail to get what I want in the Edison organization.'

"He said, 'I will see Edison, and put him on notice that I have come to go into business with him.'

"He did say, 'I will start anywhere. I will do anything Edison tells me to do, *but before I am through*, I will be his associate.'

"He said, 'There is but one thing in the world that I am determined to have, and that is a business association with Thomas A. Edison. I will burn all bridges behind me, and stake my entire future on my ability to get what I want.'"

What statements or thought patterns do you need to ditch so that your definite desire can dominate your mind?

What ships or bridges are you willing to burn so that you're not tempted to turn back? Remember: *"We win—or we perish!"*

1 _____

2 _____

3 _____

4 _____

5 _____

EXERCISE 4
Creating the Plan Confidently

Begin to carry out your desire *now*.

"[Barnes] was content to start in the most menial work, as long as it provided an opportunity to take even one step toward his cherished goal." List three concrete actions you have already taken (or are willing to take) that demonstrate your commitment to this desire.

What comes next to push your plan forward and make your desire a reality? Break down your goal into actionable steps.

_____
_____
_____
_____
_____
_____
_____
_____
_____
_____
_____
_____
_____
_____
_____
_____
_____
_____

"Whether you are ready or not, . . . put this plan into action."

EXERCISE 5
Put It All Together

Bring your desire and action plan within easy reach.

Create one statement that includes your desire and motivation (from Exercise 1) and the key steps of your action plan (from Exercise 4). If possible, use some of the passionate words from Exercise 2.

_____
_____
_____
_____
_____
_____
_____
_____
_____
_____
_____
_____
_____
_____
_____

EXERCISE 6
The Vision as Reality

Build a daily visualization habit to see your desired goal as a reality.

Dedicate ten minutes each morning and evening to visualize your desired goal as though it were already achieved. Read aloud the full statement of your burning desire and your plan to reach it (from Exercise 5). As you say the words, bring them to life. See, feel, *believe* yourself in possession of the money or goal.

Describe how it feels and what your life looks like. Try using all five senses to make the vision as vivid as possible.

EXERCISE 7
Release to Reinforce

Let go of what holds you back.

Notice how consistent visualization affects your mindset or belief in achieving your desire. If anything threatens to limit you, release it here and don't look back.

> *"If you do not see great riches in your imagination, you will never see them in your bank balance."*

2
FAITH

Develop unwavering belief in your ability to achieve your goals.

"Faith is the 'eternal elixir' which gives life, power, and action to the impulse of thought!"

When Hill met the industrial giants of his era—Carnegie, Ford, Edison—he noticed a common thread. It wasn't genius. It wasn't luck. It was faith.

They believed in themselves so completely, so resolutely, that their belief became a force of attraction. Others came to believe in them, too. Doors opened. Resources appeared. Faith didn't guarantee instant success, but it did make success inevitable. In fact, Hill said that faith is the only known antidote for failure.

In the first step toward riches, you sparked the flame. Now it's time to give it oxygen. Faith is what takes your burning desire from a hope to a conviction—from "maybe" to "must." Without it, even the strongest goals stall out. That's why Hill calls faith the "eternal elixir": It animates your desire, gives it motion and direction, and makes it believable, not just to yourself but to others and to the world around you.

You don't need to be born with a mountain of faith. Hill says faith can be created through repeated affirmation, emotion, and visualization. It is a learned mindset, not a mystical gift. And once you train your mind to believe in your goal with absolute certainty, the subconscious begins to work on it day and night, just as surely as a seed sprouts underground before the plant bursts into bloom.

Just look at the story of Barnes, who didn't just *want* to be a business associate of Edison—he *believed* he would be. And that belief carried him forward even when he started as a lowly worker, even when five years passed with no promise, and even when no one else could see it happening. The result: Barnes did exactly what he set out to do.

Faith is not just positive thinking. It is the decision to remove the possibility of failure from your consciousness. When you believe so deeply that your goal is already yours, you start to act, speak, and live like it's on its way—and the world responds in kind. In this chapter, you'll use the same tools employed by the world's wealthiest and wisest achievers to build unshakable faith in your goal through reflection, repetition, and action—until belief becomes your default setting. Carry these words of Hill in your mind: "Have Faith in yourself; Faith in the infinite."

EXERCISE 1
Speak Faith into Your Plan

Affirm your desire + belief + action daily.

Expand your statement from Chapter 1, "Desire," with this chapter's focus on faith. Write it to reflect your total belief in your ability to reach your goal. Make it strong, emotional, and personal.

Example: "I have unshakable confidence that I am earning [exact amount] by [date]. I see it. I feel it. I know it's mine. My faith is my fuel, and my plan is my proof."

Write your own statement below and track your affirmation practice each day for the week. Say it aloud twice a day. Repeat until it becomes who you are.

_____
_____
_____
_____
_____
_____
_____
_____
_____
_____

Daily Practice Tracker

	Morning	Evening
MONDAY	●	●
TUESDAY	●	●
WEDNESDAY	●	●
THURSDAY	●	●
FRIDAY	●	●
SATURDAY	●	●
SUNDAY	●	●

Continue your twice-daily affirmation practice after this week, using the tracker on page 160. Twelve additional weeks of tracking have been provided for. By then, your practice will be a habit.

> *"Repetition of affirmation of orders to your subconscious mind is the only known method of voluntary development of the emotion of faith."*

EXERCISE 2
Reverse the Doubt

Doubt dissolves when exposed to the light of truth.

What specific doubts or limiting beliefs keep popping up in your mind? List them on the left. Then, on the right, reframe them into faith-filled affirmations.

Doubt/Fear	**Faith-Filled Belief**
"I don't have enough experience."	"Every day I gain the experience I need to succeed."

"Faith is the head chemist of the mind."

EXERCISE 3
Borrowed Belief

Draw strength from others' stories of faith.

Hill admired Mahatma Gandhi, not for wealth (which he did not have) but for the way he transformed faith into a powerful force. Gandhi believed so deeply in his cause that he mobilized millions of people without weapons, armies, or riches. His belief alone—backed by persistence, clarity, and moral conviction—changed the course of history. Others have done the impossible, and so can you.

Think of someone whose story shows unwavering belief in a vision or purpose. This could be a public figure or someone you know personally. What words describe this person's faith in action? (Examples: courageous, bold, patient, focused, visionary, relentless, hopeful.)

_____

_____

_____

Which of these qualities already live in *you*?

_____

_____

_____

Which ones do you want to strengthen through faith?

_____

_____

_____

EXERCISE 4
Stronger Through Emotion

Recall past victories to fuel future ones.

Think back to three moments in your life when you believed in yourself and succeeded. Even small wins matter. Write each down with the feeling you experienced.

1

2

3

Now declare: "I've done it before. I will do it again."

EXERCISE 5
Check Your Seeds of Belief

Dig into your daily affirmations.

How is your faith-filled statement practice going? Have you been able to keep it up? Any obstacles you have faced?

_____
_____
_____

How did you feel the first time you said the words of your statement aloud? What was your body language?

_____
_____
_____

Did your confidence change after a few days of repetition?

_____
_____
_____

> *"Perfection will come through practice.*
> *It cannot come by merely reading instructions."*

EXERCISE 6
The Self-Confidence Formula

Know your worth, your power, and your ability to achieve.

Hill's five-part Self-Confidence Formula is designed to rewire your subconscious mind and build unstoppable belief in yourself. When read aloud and internalized daily, this formula becomes a mental blueprint for success. Write the entire formula out on a large piece of paper. You can use Hill's classic language from the book, the modern adaptation below, or your own desired version written on the lines.

1 I believe in my ability to achieve my greatest goal in life. That's why I commit, starting now, to taking focused, consistent action until I reach it.

_____

_____

_____

2 I understand that the thoughts I dwell on shape my reality. So each day, I'll spend thirty minutes visualizing the person I'm becoming, creating a clear mental picture of who I want to be and what I want to achieve.

_____

_____

_____

_____

3 I know that what I repeat to myself—especially with emotion—can rewire my mind and fuel my desire. So I'll take ten minutes every day to build up my confidence and remind myself of what I'm capable of.

_____

_____

_____

4 I've written down a clear, specific description of my main goal in life. I will never stop working toward it, and I'll keep building my self-confidence until I achieve it.

_____

_____

_____

5 I know that lasting success must be built on honesty, fairness, and service. I will never engage in anything that harms others. I will earn success by giving value and by earning the trust and cooperation of others. First I will believe in others—and in myself—because I understand that negative thoughts like jealousy, hate, and doubt only block success. Others will then believe in me because I show up with integrity, generosity, and confidence.

_____

_____

_____

EXERCISE 7
Begin the Build

Buy in to the power of the words to frame your thoughts.

I commit to reading the Self-Confidence Formula aloud every day for at least the next thirty days.

Start Date: _____

End Date: _____

What do you expect to change as a result of this practice?

_____

_____

_____

_____

_____

_____

_____

_____

> *"You will discover that your greatest weakness is lack of self-confidence. This handicap can be surmounted."*

3
AUTO-SUGGESTION

Influence your subconscious mind with positive self-talk.

"Any idea, plan, or purpose may be placed in the mind through repetition of thought."

Your thoughts are not idle. They are instructions. And with enough repetition and emotional intensity, they become orders to your subconscious mind.

Auto-suggestion is a technique that allows you to plant those thoughts on purpose. It's the bridge between conscious desire and unconscious belief—the daily practice of reminding your mind what you intend to accomplish and reinforcing that message until it becomes internalized truth.

Hill emphasizes that auto-suggestion is not mere wishful thinking or empty affirmation: "Plain, unemotional words do not influence the subconscious mind. You will get no appreciable results until you learn to reach your subconscious mind with thoughts or spoken words which have been well emotionalized with belief."

Auto-suggestion is *directed thought* fused with emotion and backed by purpose. You're not just saying you'll succeed—you're training yourself to believe it.

The subconscious is always listening, always recording. So when you speak your desire aloud—especially in the present tense and with conviction—you're shaping your internal blueprint. The more vivid and consistent the suggestion, the more powerfully the subconscious accepts it and begins organizing your actions, your decisions, and even your environment around it.

To use auto-suggestion effectively, you must engage your senses. Hill recommends not just *writing* your definite desire, but *reading it aloud*—morning and night—*seeing* it in your imagination, and *feeling* it as already achieved. This multisensory experience makes the goal real before it becomes visible.

Think of auto-suggestion as mental conditioning. You're training your mind the way an athlete trains a body—repetitively, deliberately, and with focused intensity. Over time, those repeated thoughts shape belief. Belief drives action. And action manifests results.

In this chapter, you'll refine your desire statement, build a powerful daily routine of repetition, and learn how to speak directly to your subconscious. Your inner world is under construction. Auto-suggestion is the tool that puts every mental brick in place.

EXERCISE 1
Reignite Your Desire Statement

Refine, recharge, and repeat with new energy.

Auto-suggestion isn't just about having a desire statement—it's about feeding it to your subconscious with emotion and belief, over and over again. It's time to check in with your original statement, make sure it still fits, and layer in new emotional depth to increase its power.

On a scale of 1–10, how emotionally connected do you feel to your desire statement today?

What's missing, if anything? Does it feel flat? Too safe? Outdated? Not vivid enough?

_____
_____
_____

If needed, adjust your statement below. Keep it bold, specific, and present tense. Now add one emotion-rich sentence that expresses why this matters. Read the entire statement aloud with fire. This becomes your new twice-daily affirmation.

_____
_____
_____
_____

EXERCISE 2
Anchoring Your Words

Emotions are the fuel behind repetition.

Repetition alone is not enough—*emotional belief* must be present. What feelings do you want to experience as you reach your goal? If you're not sure where to start, it can help to connect your desired feelings to past experiences. Give them context.

Emotion I Want to Feel	**Where I've Felt It Before**	**How I'll Connect It to My Goal**

> *"The subconscious mind recognizes and acts upon only thoughts which have been well-mixed with emotion or feeling."*

EXERCISE 3
A Daily Auto-Suggestion Ritual
Make your mental conditioning automatic.

Ritual builds habit. Habit builds belief. Belief builds results. In what designated place can you read your statement aloud each morning and evening to make it more ingrained? What visual cue or reminder can you use? How can you make the experience feel sacred, empowering, and *real*?

Morning

Time: _____

Location: _____

Visual/physical cue: _____

Emotional priming method: _____

Evening

Time: _____

Location: _____

Visual/physical cue: _____

Emotional priming method: _____

EXERCISE 4
Your Inner Dialogue

Replace unconscious suggestions with intentional ones.

Pay attention to your self-talk throughout the day. When you notice a negative or limiting thought, record it. Then rewrite it (even if it's later in the day), using the power of auto-suggestion.

Intruding Limiting Thought	**Rewritten Intentional Suggestion**
"I'm not sure this will work."	"I am confident and prepared to succeed."

> *"The subconscious mind resembl[es] a fertile garden spot, in which weeds will grow in abundance, if the seeds of more desirable crops are not sown therein."*

EXERCISE 5
Childlike Obedience

Trust the process—no overthinking, no second-guessing.

Hill encourages us to approach auto-suggestion the way a child follows instructions: with full belief, wonder, and willingness. Children don't overanalyze—they engage with heart and imagination. When they repeat something, they believe it.

For your next two affirmation practices, try adding a childlike touch.

Read your affirmation statement aloud—twice—as if you were a kid pretending it's already true. Make it fun. Smile. Believe it just for the joy of believing. Say it with playful trust, not pressure. How did that feel different from your usual approach?

_____

_____

_____

After reading your statement and doing your usual visualization, grab some crayons, markers, or pencils. Draw a simple picture of what you imagined—no need to be artistic. Let your inner child sketch out the dream.

EXERCISE 6
Walk It into Reality

Turn your affirmation into motion.

Auto-suggestion isn't just about saying the words—it's about feeling them in your body. When you move while speaking your affirmation, you engage more of your senses and strengthen the belief. Even if your ritual usually focuses on home practice, just for today, try going for a short walk (indoors or outdoors) and softly repeating your affirmation to yourself as you walk.

Say it with rhythm. Breathe with it. Match your steps to the pace of your words. Let your body carry the belief forward—literally.

What did you notice as you walked and affirmed? Did it feel different from sitting still?

_____
_____
_____
_____
_____
_____
_____
_____
_____
_____

EXERCISE 7
The Ripple Effect

Notice how repetition is changing your mindset, choices, and results.

At the end of this week, reflect on how your auto-suggestion practice is influencing your life. Have your emotions shifted? Have new ideas, people, or opportunities started appearing? Write down what you've noticed—big or small.

_____
_____
_____
_____
_____
_____
_____
_____
_____
_____

"If you try and fail, make another effort, and still another, until you succeed."

4

SPECIALIZED KNOWLEDGE

Focus on what you need relevant to your goals.

"Knowledge is only potential power. It becomes power only when, and if, it is organized into definite plans of action, and directed to a definite end."

In a world where we can access unlimited information in seconds, it's easy to confuse knowledge with wisdom—or worse, with success. But Hill makes an important distinction: General knowledge is not the key to riches. General knowledge is broad, academic, and often unused. It's only when knowledge is specialized, directed, and applied that it becomes power.

Many of the most successful people Hill studied didn't have advanced degrees or traditional credentials. What they had was a clear purpose and the drive to learn what they needed to fulfill it. They focused their attention on acquiring practical knowledge in specific areas, then used that knowledge to build something valuable.

You don't need to know everything. You just need to know what matters for your goal.

And if you don't yet know it? You can learn it, or you can organize a plan to gain it from others. You can immerse yourself in knowledge through books, mentors, partners, and even employees or advisors. The key is to stay curious and direct your learning toward your Definite Purpose. What matters is that you become the master of your mission—not by knowing everything but by assembling the knowledge and resources required. You need to become intentional about learning the things that move *your* vision forward—and surround yourself with people who can fill in the gaps.

This chapter is your chance to identify what you already know that can serve your purpose—and where you still need to grow. You'll start building a practical learning plan, explore new sources of insight, and look for ways to apply or share what you know in meaningful ways.

Specialized knowledge doesn't have to come from a classroom. It can come from a conversation, a course, a podcast, or a hard-earned life lesson. But it must be organized, acted upon, and aimed at your Definite Purpose. And it should keep expanding, rather than stagnating, so that you and your knowledge grow in ways that support your success.

This is where learning becomes power—and power becomes progress.

EXERCISE 1
The Knowledge Inventory

Identify the useful knowledge you already have.

Specialized knowledge doesn't have to come from earning a diploma. It might come from your job, your passions, your life experiences, or your side hobbies. You already carry more useful wisdom than you realize.

Write down at least five areas where you already have deep, practical, or unique knowledge.

Area of Knowledge	How You Gained It	How It Could Be Useful

What surprised you about your list?

_____
_____
_____
_____
_____

EXERCISE 2
Define the Gap

Get specific about what you still need to learn.

What kind of knowledge would move you closer to your goal right now? Rather than general facts or scattered ideas, think about specific, targeted insight that helps you take your next step. Describe the gap between where you are and where you want to be.

What specific knowledge or skill would make the biggest impact on your progress?

_____
_____
_____
_____

Where could you find that knowledge? (Books? People? Experience?)

_____
_____
_____
_____

> *"The word 'educate' is derived from the Latin word 'educo,' meaning to educe, to draw out, to develop from within."*

EXERCISE 3
Learn from the Masters

Seek out people who already know what you want to learn.

We learn from others when we're open to their offerings. Mentors, advisors, even biographies or interviews are bridges to specialized knowledge.

List three people (living or historical) who have mastered something you want to learn. Then list one way you could learn from each.

Name	What They Know	How You Can Learn from Them
_____	_____	_____
	_____	_____
	_____	_____
_____	_____	_____
	_____	_____
	_____	_____
_____	_____	_____
	_____	_____
	_____	_____

> *"Those who are not successful usually make the mistake of believing that the knowledge acquiring period ends when one finishes school."*

EXERCISE 4
Your Personal Learning Plan

Commit to acquiring specialized knowledge.

Learning is expanding. Choose one area of knowledge you want to grow in this week. Then build a focused, simple plan around it.

This week, I will focus on learning more about:

_____

_____

_____

How I'll learn:

- Reading: _____

- Online course/podcast: _____

- Shadowing/asking someone: _____

- Practicing it directly: _____

- Other: _____

One small step I can take today:

_____

_____

_____

EXERCISE 5
Applying What You Know

Put your existing knowledge to work for income, impact, or opportunity.

Knowledge has no value unless it's applied. Take what you already know and brainstorm how it could bring value to yourself or others.

List three ways your current knowledge could help you generate income, build influence, solve problems, or move forward.

What's one way you'll test or use one of these opportunities this week?

EXERCISE 6
The Master Notebook

Capture new knowledge as you go.

Success-minded people collect ideas, contacts, resources, and insights. Hill was a fan of keeping a "knowledge log" of useful, organized information. Today's assignment: Set up a notebook or digital space to capture things you learn that are relevant to your Definite Purpose.

In the space below, start by writing down three useful takeaways from Hill's specialized knowledge chapter or this week's workbook exercises on personal learning—quotes, strategies, or lessons.

What themes or patterns do you notice in what you're learning?

EXERCISE 7
Teach to Learn

Teaching deepens your understanding.

One of the fastest ways to master something is to teach it to others. When you need to explain a concept clearly, it forces you to understand it more deeply.

Choose one concept you've learned recently (from your own experience or new research). Then try explaining it simply—as if to a beginner.

Topic: _____

Explain it in two or three sentences:

_____
_____
_____
_____

Who could benefit from hearing this? Could you write a post, record a video, or share it in conversation?

_____
_____
_____
_____

5

IMAGINATION

Unlock ideas and plans to achieve success through visionary thinking.

"Man's only limitation, within reason, lies in his development and use of his imagination."

Imagination isn't just for dreamers—it's for doers. Imagination is where the invisible becomes visible.

Before any fortune was made, any invention created, or any dream realized, it existed first in someone's mind. Hill believed imagination to be one of the most powerful tools you have—because it is the workshop where all plans are forged. It's where desire transforms into vision and vision begins to shape reality.

But not all imagination is created equal. *Synthetic imagination*, the kind we use most often, rearranges existing ideas, concepts, and experiences into new combinations. It's how you solve problems creatively or improve on what already exists. *Creative imagination*, on the other hand, is the source of entirely new ideas, often arriving as sudden inspiration or insight—what Hill describes as thoughts "from beyond."

Good news: You don't have to choose between them. Start with what you know. Combine it in fresh ways. Then stay open for unexpected flashes. Imagination expands as you use it.

Most people use their imagination unconsciously—often to worry, rehearse failure, or stay stuck in old patterns. But successful people use their imagination deliberately, to design solutions, create opportunities, and rehearse success. They visualize the future with intention, believing in what they see before it materializes.

Imagination is also the cure for overwhelm. When a goal feels too big, your imagination can break it down into manageable, meaningful steps. It gives you the ability to preview progress before it's made and to practice action before you take it.

Everyone has imagination. It doesn't belong only to artists or inventors. Hill believed that the more you use your imagination with purpose, the sharper and more powerful it becomes.

In this chapter, you'll practice stretching your imagination beyond daydreams and vague hopes and into clear, intentional direction. You'll experiment with both creative and synthetic imagination—trusting that your mind is more capable, more resourceful, and more powerful than you may have realized.

You don't need to have all the answers today. You just need to imagine what's possible—and begin to build it.

EXERCISE 1
Record Your Daily Sparks

Turn imagination into a habit.

Ideas are fleeting unless you catch them. For the next seven days, jot down one idea each day—big or small—that comes to you through conversation, reading, observation, or random inspiration.

Monday

Idea/insight: _____

How I might use it: _____

Tuesday

Idea/insight: _____

How I might use it: _____

Wednesday

Idea/insight: _____

How I might use it: _____

Thursday

Idea/insight: _____

How I might use it: _____

Friday

Idea/insight: _____

How I might use it: _____

Saturday

Idea/insight: _____

How I might use it: _____

Sunday

Idea/insight: _____

How I might use it: _____

What trends or common themes do you notice?

_____

_____

_____

_____

_____

> *"On every hand one may contact stimuli which develop the imagination."*

EXERCISE 2
Reimagine the Familiar

Practice synthetic imagination by reworking existing ideas.

Innovation isn't always about creating something new—it's often about seeing something familiar in a fresh way. Choose a product, service, or system you use often. Now imagine three ways to improve it or combine it with something else.

Product/Service/System

_____

_____

_____

Your Change

_____

_____

_____

New Benefits

_____

_____

_____

EXERCISE 3
Create a Dream Collage

Give your imagination something to look at.

Create a vision board (physical or digital) that represents your goal. Include images, colors, quotes, and symbols. Don't overthink it—just pull what inspires you. Then display it where you'll see it daily.

What does your board reveal about your deepest desires?

_____
_____
_____
_____
_____
_____
_____
_____
_____
_____
_____

> *"Ideas are the beginning points of all fortunes.*
> *Ideas are products of the imagination."*

EXERCISE 4
Just the Next Step

Use your imagination to get unstuck.

If a big goal feels overwhelming, imagine only the very next step—not the entire journey. What's one next action you could take if everything were possible? Imagine doing it. Then write it out like it's already done, including the emotions you feel.

_____
_____
_____
_____
_____

How does imagining that success shift your energy or mindset?

_____
_____
_____
_____
_____

EXERCISE 5
From Impossible to Inevitable

Track real-world inventions that began as "crazy" ideas.

Hill marveled at how imagination turned the impossible into the everyday. In his time, it was airplanes, radio waves, and electricity. Today, it's things like AI, space tourism, lab-grown meat, and digital currency. Every breakthrough you see in the news started as an idea in someone's mind—an idea no more real or powerful than the one in yours.

Find a recent news story, invention, or startup that surprises you.

Headline or idea: _____

Briefly describe the innovation:

_____
_____

Why would this have seemed impossible ten or twenty years ago?

_____
_____

What does this spark in your imagination? Your idea doesn't have to be realistic—yet. Just get it on the page. Brainstorm by starting with: "I wonder if it's possible to..."

_____
_____

EXERCISE 6
Imagine It Done

Reverse engineer your goal by picturing it as already accomplished.

Sometimes the clearest ideas come not from asking, "What if?" but from asking, "What now?"—as if your goal were already complete.

1 Visualize (in vivid detail) your goal already accomplished. Picture the moment you realize: *I did it*. Where are you? What's happening? How do you feel? Describe it.

_____
_____
_____
_____
_____
_____
_____
_____
_____
_____

2 Ask yourself, *What had to happen right before this?* Then repeat the question several more times, working backward step-by-step.

Right before that, I had to . . .

_____

Before that, I needed to . . .

_____

Earlier, I chose to . . .

_____

One of the first things I did was . . .

_____

3 Record any ideas that come to light. What you've just done is map out a future-forward plan, rooted in imagination but ending with action.

_____
_____
_____
_____
_____
_____

EXERCISE 7
Let Inspiration Speak

Use creative imagination to receive ideas "out of the blue."

Set a timer for ten minutes. In silence, ask a clear question related to your goal—something you're trying to solve or unlock. Then wait. Don't force anything; just stay open. Trust that your imagination is a receiver, not just a projector.

Write down any ideas, words, or images that come to you, no matter how strange or small.

> *"The great leaders of business, industry, finance, and the great artists, musicians, poets, and writers became great, because they developed the faculty of creative imagination."*

6

ORGANIZED PLANNING

Create a concrete plan to achieve your goals and take actionable steps.

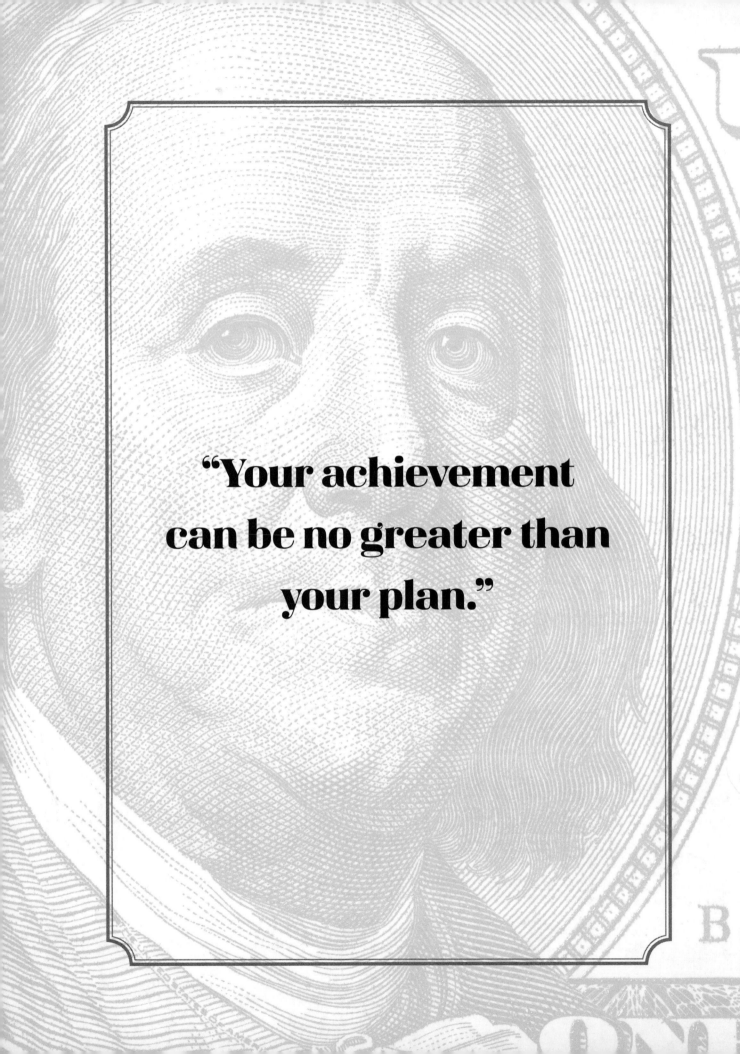

"Your achievement can be no greater than your plan."

A desire without a plan is just a wish. But a desire paired with a well-organized plan is the beginning of achievement.

By this point in the journey, you've named your goal, fueled it with belief, explored it with imagination, and drafted some first steps. Now it's time to move from the mental workshop into the real world. This is the part of the process where dreams stop floating and start walking. It's where you move from "I want to" to "Here's how I will."

Too many people stop short at the idea stage. They wait for clarity. They wait for confidence. They wait for the "perfect" path to appear. They wait for the full picture before taking a step. But success doesn't come to those who wait—it comes to those who work from a plan, even if that plan is flawed. Plans are meant to be changed and improved. What matters is that you begin.

Organized planning means breaking your goal into clear steps, setting timelines, and assigning responsibilities—starting with yourself. It also means surrounding yourself with the right people. Hill emphasizes the power of a Master Mind: a supportive team of thinkers, encouragers, mentors, and collaborators who can help you stay sharp, inspired, and accountable.

Planning also protects you from discouragement. Without a plan, a setback feels like failure. With a plan, it's just a pivot point—part of the process. And the more willing you are to revise and adapt, the more likely you are to succeed.

In this chapter, you'll move your dream into structure. You'll identify small, manageable steps. You'll set deadlines. You'll name your allies. And you'll begin practicing persistence in a way that doesn't rely on motivation—it relies on commitment.

This is your turning point: no more waiting for conditions to be perfect. As Hill says, "Put your plan into action at once." Even a simple plan carried out today is more powerful than a brilliant plan delayed forever.

EXERCISE 1
Break It Down to Build It Up

Turn your desire into action steps.

Choose one specific goal you want to focus on right now. (Consider a step to your burning desire that you outlined in Chapter 1.) Start by writing it in one clear sentence.

_____

_____

Now break it down into five smaller steps. These don't need to be perfect—just actions that move you forward.

1 _____

2 _____

3 _____

4 _____

5 _____

Which of these steps can you take this week?

_____

EXERCISE 2
Your Plan A and Plan B
Create a path—and a backup plan.

Your first plan may not work, and that's okay. The key is not to quit but to pivot. Write out a simple Plan A: the way you think your goal will unfold. Then write a Plan B: what you'll try if Plan A doesn't go as expected. Flexibility is a sign of strength—not uncertainty.

Plan A:

_____
_____
_____
_____

Plan B:

_____
_____
_____
_____

> *"Henry Ford met with temporary defeat. He created new plans, and went marching on to financial victory."*

EXERCISE 3
The Plan You Want to Follow

Design your strategy around your strengths—not just tasks.

A successful plan doesn't just check boxes—it energizes you. Your plan should match your *desire* and *personality*, not just your calendar. Designing a plan that excites you makes follow-through much more likely.

What type of work or structure brings out your best energy? (Fast-paced? Detailed? Collaborative? Flexible?)

_____
_____
_____
_____

What's one way you can build your plan around what already works for *you*?

_____
_____
_____
_____

EXERCISE 4
Deadlines Create Movement

Assign dates to your steps to build momentum.

Deadlines give plans structure—and structure gives energy. Go back to the five steps you listed in Exercise 1. Now add a realistic but firm target date to each one.

Step   **Target Date**

_____   _____

_____   _____

_____   _____

_____   _____

_____   _____

Circle the first deadline. Make it official.

"A quitter never wins—and—a winner never quits."

EXERCISE 5
Action Audit

Check in on your execution habits.

A plan is only as powerful as the action behind it. Reflect on your current habits of execution.

When you make a plan, do you usually follow through? Why or why not?

_____
_____
_____
_____

What's one habit you can change to improve your follow-through?

_____
_____
_____
_____

What's one thing you've already done this month that proves you can follow through?

_____
_____
_____
_____

EXERCISE 6
Visualize the First Win

Picture success in motion, not just in theory.

Choose one step from your plan and visualize yourself completing it successfully. Describe that moment in detail—where you are, how you feel, what it leads to: "I have just completed [step], and it felt [feeling]. The result was [outcome]."

How does this strengthen your belief in your plan?

EXERCISE 7
Your One-Page Plan

Create a simple, powerful summary you can revisit often.

Use the space below to combine your goal, your main steps, your first deadline, and your top supporters into a one-page snapshot. Post these details somewhere immediately visible (such as your mirror) or easily accessible (such as your wallet or a journal). You are now moving with organized intention.

Goal:

_____

_____

Top Three Steps:

_____

_____

_____

First Deadline:

_____

Who's Helping:

_____

_____

7

DECISION

Cultivate the ability to make firm decisions and avoid procrastination.

"The world has the habit of making room for the man whose words and actions show that he knows where he is going."

Successful people make decisions quickly—and change them slowly, if at all. Unsuccessful people hesitate, second-guess, and ask for a dozen opinions before taking even the smallest step.

Hill saw this pattern again and again in the hundreds of successful people he studied. From industrial titans to self-made inventors, they all shared a common trait: decisiveness. Not recklessness, but confident, clear action born from self-trust and a Definite Purpose.

When you're decisive, you claim your power. You stop waiting for permission, validation, or perfect timing. You choose a path—and commit to walking it. That doesn't mean you'll never adjust your course, but it means you won't waste your energy wobbling in place.

Hill believed that indecision is a form of fear—a subtle way the subconscious protects you from risk, rejection, or responsibility. But freedom and success require the courage to choose, even when the outcome isn't guaranteed. In fact, he called procrastination "the opposite of decision."

This chapter invites you to strengthen your decision-making muscles. You'll practice choosing quickly and confidently, based on your purpose—not your fears. You'll reflect on past decisions that shaped your life, and you'll identify the areas where you're still hesitating. You'll also learn how to separate instinct from insecurity, and how to trust yourself to adjust along the way.

Hill shares that many of his most successful subjects made life-altering decisions in minutes: to leave a job, start a business, or stake everything on a dream. They didn't overanalyze. They decided. And then they moved. In this chapter, you'll do the same.

It's not about getting every decision "right." It's about becoming the kind of person who takes the lead in your own life. The world responds to people who know what they want. And that power starts with your next decision.

EXERCISE 1
Decision Audit

Reflect on the role decision-making has played in your life.

Think back to a big decision you've made—one that shaped your path. It could have been about your career, a relationship, your health, or a major move.

What was the decision?

_____
_____
_____
_____
_____

How quickly did you make it?

_____
_____
_____
_____
_____

What was the result?

_____
_____
_____
_____

Would you still make that choice today? Why or why not?

_____
_____
_____
_____

Now think of a time you delayed or avoided a decision. What did indecision cost you?

_____
_____
_____
_____

> *"People who fail to accumulate money, without exception, have the habit of reaching decisions, if at all, very slowly."*

EXERCISE 2
Working the Muscle

Start building decisiveness through small daily choices.

Decisiveness is a habit—built in the same way as you build a muscle. The more you practice it, the stronger and faster your decisions become.

For the next three days, pay attention to simple choices you often overthink: What to eat. What to wear. Where to spend your time. Each time, make a decision quickly and confidently. Then reflect here. The goal isn't perfection—it's progress through clarity and commitment.

What felt different about deciding faster?

_____
_____
_____
_____

What decisions felt empowering?

_____
_____
_____
_____

EXERCISE 3
Clear the Clutter

Identify the areas where indecision is draining your energy.

Prolonged indecision leads to mental haziness and lost opportunity. But you can clear the fog with reflection and intentional practice.

List three areas in your life where you're currently undecided.

1 _____

2 _____

3 _____

Choose one. Then write the next right decision—even if it's small.

Chosen area:

_____

Decision I'm willing to make:

_____

EXERCISE 4
Decision Versus Delay

Recognize the difference between waiting and avoiding.

Sometimes we tell ourselves, "I need more time." But often, we're really avoiding risk. Write down one decision you've been putting off. What's the real reason for the delay? Be honest.

The decision:

_____
_____
_____
_____
_____
_____

What I tell myself:

_____
_____
_____
_____
_____
_____

What might really be going on:

_____
_____
_____
_____
_____
_____
_____
_____

Now finish this sentence: "If I trusted myself more, I would..."

_____
_____
_____
_____
_____
_____
_____
_____

> *"Those who reach decisions promptly and definitely, know what they want, and generally get it."*

EXERCISE 5
Decide in Alignment

Use your Definite Purpose as your compass.

Not every opportunity deserves your "yes." Use your Definite Purpose as a filter for choices.

One decision you're currently considering:

_____
_____
_____
_____

How does it support (or distract from) your definite goal?

_____
_____
_____
_____

What would someone already living your desired life choose in this situation?

_____
_____
_____
_____

EXERCISE 6
Burn the Bridge (When Needed)

Commit fully by removing the escape route.

Successful people make bold decisions and cut off all possibility of retreat. Is there a decision in your life where you've been "half-in"? Where you're still keeping one foot in the past?

Name it:

_____
_____
_____
_____

What would it look like to fully commit? What "bridge" might you need to burn to move forward?

_____
_____
_____
_____

> *"Definiteness of decision always requires courage, sometimes very great courage."*

EXERCISE 7
Your Decision Declaration

Affirm your ability to decide with confidence and clarity.

Write a short, powerful statement you can repeat when you're faced with hesitation.

Examples:

- "I make clear, confident decisions in alignment with my goals."
- "I act quickly on what matters and release what doesn't."
- "I trust myself to choose wisely—and adjust when needed."

Now write your own:

_____
_____
_____
_____
_____
_____

Repeat it aloud every morning for the next seven days. You are becoming the kind of person who leads with clarity, courage, and conviction.

8

PERSISTENCE

Push forward despite challenges and setbacks.

"Without persistence, you will be defeated, even before you start. With persistence you will win."

Persistence is the fire that keeps your desire burning long after the initial excitement fades. It's what separates those who succeed from those who simply wish for success. Hill considered persistence the glue that holds all the other principles together. Without it, even the clearest goals, the boldest decisions, and the most brilliant plans eventually fizzle out.

The challenge: Persistence doesn't always feel powerful. It often shows up looking like repetition despite rejection, or resilience in the face of silence. It's easy to keep going when results come quickly. It's much harder when the payoff is invisible, or when the path feels lonely, slow, or uncertain.

That's why Hill believed persistence is a habit—not a personality trait. It can be built, strengthened, and called upon. And every time you choose to show up, push forward, or try again, you're training that habit.

In fact, Hill writes that many people quit just inches from victory—not because their plan was wrong but because they stopped too soon. His encouragement is clear: You don't fail when you fall. You fail when you quit.

In this chapter, you'll look at what persistence means in your own life. You'll explore what tends to shake your commitment, and how to push through those moments. You'll also learn to tie your persistence to purpose—because when your "why" is strong, your willingness to endure grows stronger, too.

You'll build strategies to stay consistent even when you don't feel like it. And you'll begin to measure success not just by results but by the habit of continuing.

This is the chapter where grit meets grace. Where effort becomes endurance. Where you prove to yourself—and to the world—that you are the kind of person who follows through. And that, Hill assures us, is what makes all the difference.

EXERCISE 1
Your "Why" That Won't Quit

Strengthen your persistence by reconnecting to purpose.

Persistence grows when you know what you're fighting for.

What's the goal you're working toward right now?

_____
_____
_____
_____

Why does this goal truly matter to you—not just at the surface, but deep down? Ask yourself five times, each time going deeper.

Why do I want this?

_____
_____
_____

Why does that matter to me?

_____
_____
_____

And why is that important?

_____
_____
_____

What happens if I don't pursue this?

_____
_____
_____
_____

What changes if I stay committed?

_____
_____
_____
_____

Write your final, fire-starting reason below:

_____
_____
_____
_____

EXERCISE 2
What Stops You?

Identify the moments when persistence tends to break.

Most people stop short of success because they hit a wall and assume it's the end. But persistence turns walls into detours—not dead ends. Recognizing your personal obstacles helps you prepare for them. Think back to a time you gave up on something you wanted, and dig into what got in the way.

What was the goal?

_____

_____

_____

_____

What caused you to quit or pause?

_____

_____

_____

_____

How might you respond differently now?

_____

_____

_____

_____

EXERCISE 3
Reframe Rejection and Setbacks

Turn disappointment into fuel.

Hill shares stories of people who were rejected dozens—even hundreds—of times before they succeeded. What separated them from people who gave up? Persistence.

Write about a recent setback or "no" you experienced. Be honest. What happened?

_____

_____

_____

_____

Now reframe it. What could this experience teach you? How can it make you stronger, smarter, or more focused?

_____

_____

_____

_____

> *"A few carry on despite all opposition. These few are the Fords, Carnegies, Rockefellers, and Edisons."*

EXERCISE 4
Build a Persistence Ritual

Create a simple system to stay committed daily.

Persistence isn't powered by motivation—it's built through habit. Choose one action you can take every day for the next seven days that supports your goal.

Daily action:

When and where will you do it?

> *"If you find yourself lacking in persistence, this weakness may be remedied by building a stronger fire under your desires."*

Track Your Consistency

	Completed
DAY 1	●
DAY 2	●
DAY 3	●
DAY 4	●
DAY 5	●
DAY 6	●
DAY 7	●

What did you learn about your consistency this week?

_____
_____
_____
_____
_____
_____
_____
_____
_____
_____

EXERCISE 5
Stories of Grit

Draw inspiration from persistent people.

Think of someone (living or historical) who kept going against the odds—whether in business, sports, creativity, or everyday life.

Who is it? What did they persist through?

_____

_____

_____

What part of their story inspires you most?

_____

_____

_____

What lesson can you apply to your own goal this week?

_____

_____

_____

EXERCISE 6
The Ten-Minute Push

When you want to quit, keep going a little longer.

Many people quit right before a breakthrough. Next time you feel like giving up on a task or practice, set a timer for ten more minutes. Just keep going. Often, what seems unbearable becomes manageable once you push past resistance. Try it this week, then record what happened.

What were you doing?

_____
_____
_____

How did the extra ten minutes feel?

_____
_____
_____

What did you learn about yourself?

_____
_____
_____

EXERCISE 7
Declare Who You Are

Affirm your identity as someone who follows through.

Persistence becomes easier when you stop seeing it as *something you do* and start seeing it as *who you are*. Write a short declaration you can repeat out loud every day to reinforce your persistence mindset. Let it remind you who you're becoming.

Examples:

- "I am the kind of person who keeps going—no matter what."
- "I do not stop when it's hard. I adjust and continue."
- "Persistence is my power."

Your declaration:

___

"Persistence is a state of mind, therefore it can be cultivated."

9
THE MASTER MIND

Surround yourself with people who support and contribute to your success.

"Advantages may be created by any person who surrounds himself with the advice, counsel, and personal cooperation of a group who are willing to lend him wholehearted aid."

If you're trying to build success all on your own, you're working too hard—and limiting your potential. No significant achievement happens in isolation. Every great fortune, invention, business, or movement can be traced back to the power of collaborative thinking—what Hill calls Master Mind.

A Master Mind isn't just a group of advisors. It's the energetic and intellectual synergy created when two or more minds come together in harmony to work toward a Definite Purpose. It's not about collecting opinions—it's about creating momentum.

Hill believed this force was so powerful it actually created a "third mind," greater than the sum of its parts. Your thinking expands when you intentionally surround yourself with people who challenge, sharpen, support, and stretch you. You gain insight you couldn't access alone. You move faster. You course-correct sooner. You grow more confidently.

The key is harmony. Your Master Mind shouldn't be made up of random voices or passive cheerleaders. You want aligned, committed individuals who bring energy, honesty, and expertise to the table—people who want to see you win and are willing to speak the truth to help you get there.

In this chapter, you'll reflect on who's currently in your "thinking circle," identify who might be missing, and begin building or refining your own Master Mind group. You'll also learn how to become a powerful Master Mind partner for someone else, because it's not just about what you receive. It's about what you give.

You don't need dozens of people. Even one or two focused minds can make a powerful difference if you meet with intention, consistency, and shared vision. The most successful people make these relationships a nonnegotiable part of their routine.

You don't have to go it alone. In fact, you *shouldn't*. With the right people around you, your potential multiplies.

EXERCISE 1
Inventory of Your Inner Circle

Evaluate who's influencing your thinking.

The people around us either lift us higher or weigh us down. Your current circle may be shaping your future more than you realize.

List the five people you spend the most time with (personally or professionally):

1. _____

2. _____

3. _____

4. _____

5. _____

Now reflect: Whose mindset challenges you to grow?

_____
_____
_____
_____

Who energizes you? Who drains you?

_____
_____
_____
_____

Who believes in your goal—and reminds you of your potential?

_____
_____
_____
_____

What patterns do you notice?

_____
_____
_____
_____

EXERCISE 2
Identify the Gaps

Get clear on what kinds of minds you need around you.

Your Master Mind should help fill in what you lack—skills, experience, confidence, strategy, or perspective.

What are three areas where you could use more support, insight, or accountability?

1 _____

2 _____

3 _____

Now brainstorm the type of person (or specific people) who could help in each area.

Need/Gap	Ideal Support	Where to Find

EXERCISE 3
Design Your Dream Master Mind

Create a vision for your ideal support team.

If you could assemble a three-to-five-person Master Mind to help you achieve your biggest goal, who would be there? They can be people you already know, people you hope to meet, or even imagined "advisors" based on people you admire.

Name	Role	What They Bring

What would your life look like if you had this team in place?

_____
_____
_____
_____
_____
_____

EXERCISE 4
Identify and Invite

Take the first step to building your Master Mind.

Who's one person you could reach out to this week to begin building your Master Mind? It might be a friend, mentor, colleague, or someone you admire.

Name: _____

What you appreciate about them:

_____
_____
_____
_____

How you'll approach them:

_____
_____
_____
_____

Draft a short message to invite a conversation about collaboration, support, or even forming a group. Then don't delay in getting it out! Remember: People are often waiting for the invitation to connect with purpose.

> *"It is a well known fact that a group of electric batteries will provide more energy than a single battery."*

EXERCISE 5
Strengthen Another's Vision

Be the kind of partner you'd want in your Master Mind.

Finding a great Master Mind partner isn't just about receiving help—it's about giving help as well. Persistence shared is persistence multiplied. Who in your life is working toward something important? What could you do this week to encourage them, offer insight, or ask a thoughtful question that helps them grow?

Name: _____

Their goal:

_____
_____
_____
_____

My encouragement or support:

_____
_____
_____
_____

EXERCISE 6
Commit to Connection

Make Master Mind relationships part of your routine.

Regular and consistent meetings with your Master Mind group will drive you all forward through inspiration and accountability. It doesn't have to be formal; it just has to be intentional.

What rhythm would work best for you?

- Weekly 1:1 calls
- Monthly sessions
- Quarterly strategy check-ins
- Accountability check-ins via text or email
- Your custom idea: _____

What's one action you'll take this week to put that rhythm in motion?

_____
_____
_____
_____
_____

EXERCISE 7
Your Master Mind Manifesto

Affirm your commitment to connection and collaboration.

Write a short manifesto—an intention you'll live by as you build your Master Mind network.

You can include your values (such as honesty, encouragement, accountability), your purpose, and how you want to show up for others. Read this aloud any time you need to remind yourself: You don't have to do it alone.

Examples:

- "I will surround myself with people who sharpen my thinking and strengthen my purpose."

- "I give and receive support freely, knowing we rise higher together."

- "I will create a space where success is shared and truth is welcome."

_____
_____
_____
_____
_____
_____
_____
_____

10

THE MYSTERY OF SEX TRANSMUTATION

Channel powerful energy into creative and productive outlets.

"When driven by this desire, men develop keenness of imagination, courage, will-power, persistence, and creative ability unknown to them at other times."

This chapter may have the most mysterious title, but the idea at its core is both practical and powerful: Your desire for connection and intimacy is a potent creative force to be harnessed.

Hill believed that sexual energy, when redirected toward a higher purpose, becomes one of the greatest drivers of imagination, persistence, charisma, and achievement. It's not about suppression; it's about transformation. Hill called this process transmutation, or converting one form of energy into another.

He observed that many of the most successful people he studied had unusually high levels of passion, magnetism, and drive. And he noted that this powerful energy often stemmed from what he called "sex energy"—not in a purely physical sense, but in its broader emotional and creative dimensions.

What he's really pointing to is this: You have a wellspring of emotional, physical, and spiritual energy within you. And when you learn to channel it intentionally, it fuels greatness.

This principle goes beyond sexuality. It's about desire—not just for people but for life, love, meaning, and expression. It's about harnessing what stirs your soul and focusing that into action. Hill believed this is the source of genius: not cold logic but emotional intensity guided by purpose.

In this chapter, you'll explore what truly ignites you, where your deepest passions lie, and how to direct that energy into your mission. You'll reflect on how you use your energy—creatively, relationally, or otherwise—and where it might be scattered or misdirected. Most importantly, you'll learn how to reclaim your vitality and use it to fuel your imagination, commitment, and courage.

Sex transmutation isn't about denying your desire. It's about raising it to something even greater.

EXERCISE 1
Energy Leak Check-In

Find out what's draining you—and cut the cord.

We all have energy, but not all of us use it well. Creative power is often scattered through worry, frustration, distractions, unfulfilling habits, or unresolved emotional tension. When we plug those leaks, we reclaim strength and clarity. Take an honest inventory of where your emotional or physical energy is leaking right now.

List three people, habits, thoughts, or situations that drain or misuse your energy.

1 _____

2 _____

3 _____

What emotion tends to accompany each energy drain (guilt, anxiety, boredom, resentment)?

_____
_____
_____
_____

What boundaries, shifts, or decisions could help close the energy leaks?

_____
_____
_____
_____
_____
_____

What's one thing you can say "no" to this week to protect your energy?

_____
_____
_____
_____
_____
_____

What's one thing you want to say "yes" to instead—something that brings joy, focus, or creative fire?

_____
_____
_____
_____
_____
_____

EXERCISE 2
The Magnetism List

Recognize how passion makes you more magnetic.

Hill noticed that those who transmuted their energy developed greater personal magnetism—a natural charisma that attracted people, ideas, and resources.

What traits do you find magnetic in others?

_____

_____

Now flip it: What makes *you* magnetic when you're fully alive and purpose-driven? List five traits that emerge in you when you're lit up from within.

1 _____

2 _____

3 _____

4 _____

5 _____

These are your high-frequency states. Find ways to operate from them more often.

EXERCISE 3
The Spark Behind the Spark

Look at who or what inspires your energy—and why.

Sexual transmutation isn't about waiting for inspiration to strike. It's about recognizing what already stirs your soul and learning to harness that energy on command. Think about someone or something that stirs a powerful feeling in you. It might be a person you love or admire, a piece of music, or a personal memory. Whatever it is, it lights you up.

What does this person or thing represent to you?

_____

_____

_____

What qualities do they draw out of you that make you feel most alive?

_____

_____

_____

What does this reveal about what you most long to express or create?

_____

_____

_____

EXERCISE 4
Cultivate Creative Fire

Unlock genius born from intense desire.

Think back to a moment when you felt focused, inspired, productive, and fully alive. Something moved through you that felt bigger than routine effort. That's the creative fire Hill is talking about. Use the prompts below to reconnect with that moment—and explore how to cultivate it more often.

Describe a moment when you were creatively "on fire."

_____
_____
_____
_____
_____

What sparked it? Where were you directing your energy at the time?

_____
_____
_____

How can you re-create those conditions more often?

_____
_____
_____

EXERCISE 5
Inspire Before You Create

Tap into beauty or desire to elevate your work.

Hill believed that many of history's great thinkers, artists, and inventors were inspired not by logic but by love, admiration, or aesthetic energy. They let passion raise their creative standards. Before your next creative task (writing, building, planning, etc.), take five minutes to engage with something that inspires or stirs you: a piece of music, a photo, a poem, a memory, or even the thought of someone who moves you deeply.

What did you choose to inspire you?

_____

_____

_____

What feelings or images did it awaken?

_____

_____

_____

How did it affect your mindset or creative output?

_____

_____

_____

EXERCISE 6
Ignite Your Vision

Infuse your vision board with passion, purpose, and creative energy.

Earlier in this workbook, you created a vision board—a visual representation of the life you're building. Now it's time to give it heat. Hill believed that emotionally charged desire is the fuel that turns dreams into reality. The more feeling, intensity, and personal meaning you attach to your vision, the more magnetic and motivating it becomes.

In this exercise, you'll revisit your board and layer in the energy Hill called "sex energy"—not in a romantic sense but as the most powerful form of creative, emotional, and expressive force you can generate.

Take ten to fifteen minutes to reflect on the following questions, then update your board with images, colors, words, or symbols that reflect passion, intensity, beauty, creativity, and love.

What on your board already stirs something deep in you? What gives you butterflies, goose bumps, or fire-in-the-belly excitement?

_____

_____

_____

_____

_____

What parts feel flat, incomplete, or purely logical? How could you make them more emotionally alive?

_____
_____
_____
_____
_____
_____
_____

What desires (romantic, artistic, spiritual, or personal) have you been afraid to express visually—but belong there?

_____
_____
_____
_____
_____
_____
_____

Now, gather or create three new elements to add to your board. Choose things that symbolize not just what you want but how you want to feel as you create it.

Stick them on. Sit with the board. Let it pulse with desire. This is your reminder: Success doesn't come from rational planning alone. It comes from a vision that stirs your soul—and calls your full energy forward.

EXERCISE 7
Transmutation in Practice

Make this principle part of your real daily life.

How will you begin to redirect your emotional and physical energy toward your highest goals this week? Write a short commitment below. Be specific. Let this be the beginning of a lifelong habit of fueling your greatness with the energy that already lives inside you.

Examples:

- "I will use my morning energy to create instead of scroll."
- "I will take the energy from relationship stress and pour it into writing my business plan."
- "I will move my body to activate creative flow."

Your commitment:

_____
_____
_____
_____

"The mind responds to stimulation!"

11
THE SUBCONSCIOUS MIND

Master your subconscious mind to align with your goals.

"The subconscious mind will not remain idle! If you fail to plant desires in your subconscious mind, it will feed upon the thoughts which reach it as the result of your neglect."

Think of your subconscious mind as the soil where your thoughts take root. Whether you plant something intentionally or not, *something* will grow. That's why Hill warns us that the subconscious never rests. It's always working—either for you or against you.

Our best move is to become deliberate gardeners of the mind. Whatever is repeated often enough—especially with emotion and belief—sinks below the surface and begins shaping our habits, our instincts, our creativity, and even our perception of what's possible. Thoughts backed by strong feeling become internalized instructions. And those instructions guide our words, actions, and results.

The subconscious doesn't filter for truth or logic. It accepts whatever it's told—over and over—especially when that input is emotionally charged. So if you constantly repeat doubt, fear, or failure, your subconscious will start making those outcomes feel inevitable. But when you consistently speak belief, purpose, and possibility? That's when everything changes.

Hill believed the subconscious mind is the bridge between desire and action, the connector between your conscious goals and the deeper part of you that governs 90 percent of your decisions. The more closely you align your subconscious thoughts with your Definite Purpose, the faster and more powerfully your progress accelerates.

In this chapter, you'll learn to communicate intentionally with your subconscious. You'll reinforce the thoughts you want to grow. You'll pay attention to the inner stories you've been repeating without realizing it. And you'll begin to replace unhelpful mental patterns with new ones rooted in faith, desire, and vision.

You are always programming your subconscious mind. So make sure what you're programming is helping you rise.

EXERCISE 1
Tune In to Your Inner Track

Discover the thoughts you repeat without realizing it.

Take a day to observe your inner voice. When you're quiet, stuck, trying something hard, or making a decision, what do you hear?

List five common thoughts or phrases you catch yourself thinking.

1. _____
2. _____
3. _____
4. _____
5. _____

Now go back and label each one: Uplifting (U), Neutral (N), or Limiting (L).

How many of your most common thoughts are actually helping you?

_____

EXERCISE 2
Rewrite the Script

Turn negative patterns into positive programming.

Take one limiting thought from Exercise 1 and rewrite it into a new, empowering belief. Repetition is the key to making this new script stick.

Old thought:

_____

_____

_____

New belief:

_____

_____

_____

Now write your new belief again—slowly, with intention.

_____

_____

_____

Say it aloud whenever you feel the old thoughts and patterns hovering. Your mind believes what it hears most often.

EXERCISE 3
Food for Your Mind

Your input becomes your internal programming.

Just as your body reflects what you eat, your mind reflects the information you consume. Your subconscious is always taking in, so it's your job to choose what it gets most often.

List three sources you regularly expose your mind to—news, social media, conversations, entertainment, etc.

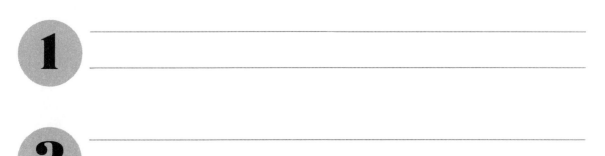

1. _____

2. _____

3. _____

What messages are those inputs sending you? Are they aligned with your goals and purpose?

Now list three intentional sources of inspiration or truth you want to feed your subconscious from instead.

1 _____

2 _____

3 _____

What's one thing you'll eliminate or limit this week to protect your mental soil?

_____
_____
_____
_____
_____
_____

> *"Positive and negative emotions cannot occupy the mind at the same time."*

EXERCISE 4
Subconscious Gratitude Script

Use gratitude to train your inner mind toward abundance.

Gratitude isn't just a feel-good practice. It's a powerful way to teach your subconscious to look for what's working. And when you look for what's working, you begin to expect more of it.

Write a gratitude script as if everything you desire were already happening. Use present tense and emotionally charged language.

Example:
"I am so grateful for the clarity and momentum I feel each morning. I'm attracting incredible opportunities and support. My mind is focused and powerful."

Now write your own:

_____

_____

_____

Read your gratitude script a few times through aloud. How does it affect your focus or feelings?

_____

_____

_____

_____

EXERCISE 5
Program Your Night Mind

Use sleep as a tool for subconscious alignment.

The subconscious works especially well while you sleep, so harness that power. While your head rests on your pillow, let your dreams do some of the work.

Right before bed tonight, focus on your gratitude script from Exercise 4. Write it out again below. Then read it aloud, slowly and confidently.

_____
_____
_____

Close your eyes and visualize the statement as if it's already real. What do you see? How do you feel? What does life look like in that version of reality?

Do this every night this week. Then reflect on how it feels and what you learn.

_____
_____
_____
_____
_____
_____

EXERCISE 6
The Power Phrase

Create a go-to statement to interrupt negative thought spirals.

Sometimes you need a phrase you can grab in the moment—something short, strong, and familiar to interrupt worry, self-doubt, or overthinking.

Examples:

- "I choose faith over fear."
- "This thought doesn't serve my future."
- "Reset. Refocus. Rise."

When do you most need a power phrase? (Think: moments of stress, procrastination, fear, distraction, etc.)

_____

_____

_____

What kind of energy do you want this phrase to bring—calm, strength, courage, focus?

_____

_____

_____

Create your own power phrase:

___

___

___

Where can you keep your power phrase visible this week? Sticky note, phone lock screen, mirror, journal?

___

___

___

Use your phrase in the next twenty-four hours. What happens when you say it? How do your body and thoughts respond?

___

___

___

___

___

___

> *"It is your responsibility to make sure that positive emotions constitute the dominating influence of your mind."*

EXERCISE 7
Speak to Your Inner Self

Send a message to let your subconscious know what kind of story you're writing.

Imagine your subconscious is a younger version of you—open, curious, and listening closely. What do you want that part of you to believe?

Write a short message to your subconscious mind—full of belief, truth, and love. Make it present tense and deeply personal.

Example:
"You are strong. You are capable. You are designed for meaningful success. Everything you need is already within you."

_____

_____

_____

_____

Now write your statement again on a separate piece of paper and keep it in a place where you can easily access it when doubts arise.

> *"Faith and fear make poor bedfellows.*
> *Where one is found, the other cannot exist."*

12
THE BRAIN

Recognize your mind as both transmitter and receiver to attract opportunities.

"Every human brain is both a broadcasting and receiving station for the vibration of thought."

You've already learned that thoughts are powerful. But Hill believed the brain doesn't just create thoughts—it transmits and receives them like a radio tower. With emotion as the amplifier and repetition as the tuning dial, your brain becomes one of the most powerful tools for success you'll ever use.

In Hill's time, this idea seemed revolutionary. But modern science has caught up. We now know the brain is deeply responsive to input, capable of forming new pathways, tuning in to emotional frequencies, and changing its structure through intention and repetition—a phenomenon known as neuroplasticity.

Hill taught that when your brain is charged with desire, faith, and persistence, it becomes magnetized. You start attracting people, ideas, and opportunities that match the frequency of your dominant thoughts. In essence, your mind becomes a magnet—not just for solutions but for the resources and allies that will help bring your goals to life.

But just like a radio, your brain can also pick up the wrong station—fear, distraction, or negativity. That's why Hill emphasized the importance of controlling your emotional state and focusing on thoughts that align with your Definite Purpose.

In this chapter, you'll begin to notice what "frequency" you're broadcasting most often—and how to tune it with clarity and intention. You'll reflect on what kinds of thoughts and emotions dominate your day, and how that affects what you're picking up from the world around you. You'll also practice consciously charging your brain with energy, emotion, and high-level thinking to increase creativity, connection, and personal magnetism.

Your brain is not just a storage unit. It's a sending and receiving station—and you control the dial.

EXERCISE 1
What Are You Transmitting?

Identify the dominant thought you're sending out into the world.

Your brain is constantly broadcasting your most frequent and emotionally charged thoughts. Those thoughts, over time, begin to shape your experiences.

What's a thought or belief you've been "transmitting" lately through your words, energy, or actions?

_____

_____

_____

Is this thought aligned with your goal or working against it?

_____

_____

_____

What new thought do you want to send? Write it in present tense, with clarity and confidence.

_____

_____

_____

EXERCISE 2
Tune Your Frequency

Adjust your mental "station" for better results.

You can't expect clear results if you're tuned in to the wrong mental channel. This week, pay attention to what kind of "signal" you're putting out. What kind of energy do you want to broadcast each day this week?

Desired Energy/Thought

Monday _____

Tuesday _____

Wednesday _____

Thursday _____

Friday _____

Saturday _____

Sunday _____

How does it feel to choose your frequency instead of falling into one?

_____
_____
_____

EXERCISE 3
Receiving Mode

Strengthen your ability to receive creative ideas.

The brain doesn't just send ideas; it receives them, too. You can't always force inspiration, but you can prepare to receive it.

Choose a quiet moment today. Sit still. Breathe deeply. Then ask your mind: *What idea, insight, or answer wants to come through right now?*

Let the silence speak. Then write what you receive.

_____

_____

_____

_____

_____

Repeat this practice two or three times this week. You're learning to trust what's being broadcast to you, not just what you send out.

> *"Man has depended too much upon his physical senses, and has limited his knowledge to physical things."*

EXERCISE 4
Power Up with Emotion

Charge your thoughts with emotional energy.

Thoughts become "magnetized" when you add emotion to them. A thought plus a feeling is what your brain responds to most. Choose a goal you're working on, then identify the emotional energy that would best fuel it.

Goal: _____

Emotion to pair with it: _____

What action could you take today that reinforces that emotion?

_____
_____
_____
_____
_____
_____
_____
_____
_____
_____

EXERCISE 5
Sync with Your Master Mind

Sharpen your brain by tapping into others'.

The brain becomes more powerful when connected with other minds working toward a shared goal. A great conversation can unlock insight, renew motivation, or reveal the next step you couldn't see on your own. Don't underestimate what one aligned exchange can do.

Reach out to a member of your Master Mind group—or someone who shares your purpose—and talk through a challenge or idea.

With whom will you connect? _____

What will you share or ask? _____

What insight or energy do you hope to gain from that exchange?

_____
_____
_____
_____
_____
_____
_____
_____
_____

EXERCISE 6
Upgrade Your Input

Feed your brain what you want to multiply.

The brain receives input constantly—from conversations, headlines, media, environments. That input becomes your thoughts.

List three things you consumed this week that left you drained or scattered:

1 _____

2 _____

3 _____

Now list three sources that lifted, inspired, or sharpened you:

1 _____

2 _____

3 _____

What will you remove or reduce going forward? What will you invite more of? You get to choose the frequency you live on.

_____

EXERCISE 7
Thought Hygiene

Declutter your mental space.

Just as your physical environment affects your focus, your mental environment shapes your energy. The brain can't operate at its highest level when flooded with worry, noise, or negative repetition. Take a few minutes to notice what thoughts you've been replaying on a loop.

What's the noisiest or most repetitive thought in your mind this week?

_____
_____
_____
_____

Is it helpful or harmful to your purpose?

_____
_____
_____
_____

Now write a replacement thought—one that clears space and realigns your focus.

_____
_____
_____
_____

13

THE SIXTH SENSE

Tap into your intuition and develop a deeper understanding of life and success.

"Through the aid of the sixth sense, you will be warned of impending dangers in time to avoid them, and notified of opportunities in time to embrace them."

This principle may be the most mysterious and, in many ways, the most profound. It cannot be fully explained by science or logic. Yet, time and again, Hill saw its power in the lives of the most successful people he studied.

The Sixth Sense, as Hill defines it, is an intuitive faculty that emerges after you've mastered the other twelve principles. It is not a shortcut or a secret hack but the quiet reward of deep alignment. When your desire is clear, your plans are in motion, your mind is focused, and your energy is aligned, a new kind of insight begins to surface.

You start sensing the next right move before it's obvious. You receive ideas that feel like they didn't come *from* you, but *through* you. You feel nudges, gut instincts, or flashes of inspiration that bypass logic—and yet prove to be true.

Hill believed the Sixth Sense is how we access infinite intelligence—that greater field of wisdom, creativity, and connection beyond conscious reasoning. You can't force it to show up. But you can create the conditions for it to rise.

In this final chapter, you'll reflect on times you've experienced intuition or unexpected guidance. You'll learn to recognize the subtle voice of your inner knowing. And you'll begin to develop a relationship with the part of you that sees more than your eyes can.

The Sixth Sense is the reward for the inner work you've done. It's the whisper behind the wisdom. It's the signal that guides you forward, even when the map isn't clear.

You've built the foundation. Now listen for the insight that comes only when you're fully aligned and ready to receive.

EXERCISE 1
Trusting the Unseen Signal

Recall a moment when intuition led you.

The Sixth Sense often shows up as a hunch, a gut feeling, or a flash of knowing. Before logic kicks in, before evidence shows up, there's a nudge that says, "This is the way." Sometimes the clearest way to trust your inner wisdom *now* is to remember how well it served you *before*.

Think of a time when you acted on instinct or insight—whether in a big decision or a subtle moment that turned out to matter—before you had logical proof.

What happened?

_____
_____
_____
_____
_____

What did you feel or sense?

_____
_____
_____
_____
_____

What did you choose to do?

_____

_____

_____

_____

What was the outcome?

_____

_____

_____

_____

Looking back, what do you think was guiding you in that moment?

_____

_____

_____

_____

> *"Eventually you will find yourself in possession of a power that will enable you to throw off discouragement, master fear, overcome procrastination, and draw freely upon your imagination."*

EXERCISE 2
Create Quiet Space

Make room for insight to surface.

The Sixth Sense rarely speaks over noise. It shows up in stillness, focus, and emotional alignment. Take ten minutes today to sit quietly—no phone, no music, no multitasking, no agenda. Just breathe, observe, and allow space for something deeper to arise.

Afterward, jot down any images, ideas, words, or feelings that came through. Even better—repeat this for a few days. Insight builds with consistency. What patterns, whispers, or signals begin to emerge? This is the practice of hearing what's already within you.

EXERCISE 3
Ask, Then Listen

Use your inner guidance to get unstuck.

Sometimes the answers we need aren't "out there." They're already inside, waiting for us to quiet down and ask the right question. Hill believed that the Sixth Sense becomes active when the conscious and subconscious minds are aligned and open to receive. This is your chance to practice listening beyond logic.

Think of a decision or challenge you're facing. Write it out in the form of a clear, focused question. Then take a few deep breaths, sit with the question, ask it aloud or in your mind, and just listen. You might receive a word, an image, a pull toward action, or a quiet sense of knowing.

Your question: _____

What came to you (idea, phrase, image, feeling)?

_____

_____

_____

What's one small action you could take based on this?

_____

_____

_____

EXERCISE 4
Your Signal Language

Notice how the Sixth Sense speaks to you.

Some people feel intuition in their body (a gut feeling, a chill). Others hear a phrase, see an image, or feel an unexplainable calm or pull. Your job is to learn your own "signal language." Think of two or three moments when your intuition was right.

What did it feel like? What did your body or mind do? What symbols or signals tend to show up for you?

_____
_____
_____
_____
_____
_____
_____
_____

"Understanding of the sixth sense comes only by meditation through mind development from within."

EXERCISE 5
Open to the Unseen

Let insight arise through creative flow.

Hill said creative imagination is the receiving set for Infinite Intelligence. One way to tap into it is through creative, nonlinear activity. Choose one of the following: doodle, write a poem, free journal, paint, collage, or take a walk with no destination. Then write down any idea or sensation that bubbled up during or after the activity. You don't have to understand your intuition fully. You just have to stay open to it.

What activity did you choose?

_____

_____

_____

_____

What surfaced that felt unexpected or wise?

_____

_____

_____

_____

_____

EXERCISE 6
Your Invisible Council
Use Hill's famous technique for inspired guidance.

Hill imagined a personal Invisible Council of historical figures and mentors—people he admired and learned from. In his mind, he'd meet with them for advice. Create your own mental council. Choose three to five people (living or passed, real or imagined) whose values or wisdom you trust.

Name	Why Chosen	What They Might Advise

Picture a conversation with your Invisible Council about your current goal. What might they say?

_____
_____
_____
_____

EXERCISE 7
Affirm the Connection

Strengthen your trust in your inner wisdom.

Write a short affirmation that reminds you to trust your Sixth Sense—even when logic lags behind. Repeat it any time you feel doubt, and watch what arises in its place.

Examples:

- "I am deeply connected to guidance beyond what I can see."
- "My intuition is clear, trustworthy, and aligned with my purpose."
- "I move with confidence in the direction of inner knowing."

Now write yours in big, bold letters:

Congratulations, You Did the Work

And now the work begins again, with more clarity, confidence, and purpose.

You've walked through all thirteen principles of Napoleon Hill's *Think and Grow Rich*—not just reading about them but living them. You've clarified your desire, fueled your faith, learned the power of persistence, built a plan, tuned your thinking, and even practiced listening for unseen guidance.

Hill reminded us often: Knowledge is not power—*applied* knowledge is. And that's exactly what you've done.

This workbook wasn't about rushing to riches or chasing someone else's definition of success. It was about helping you build a solid foundation—one rooted in intentional thought, creative energy, aligned action, and belief in your own potential.

Maybe you didn't get every page perfect. Maybe you paused, restarted, skipped a day, or wrestled with doubt. That's okay. What matters most is that you kept showing up. That's what growth looks like.

Now it's up to you to continue using these principles—not just when things are going well, but especially when momentum dips or fear creeps in. Revisit the exercises. Refresh your desire. Recommit to your purpose. And most importantly, trust yourself.

You've developed tools for clarity, consistency, and creative power. You've practiced persistence. You've connected with your imagination, your subconscious, and your intuitive mind. You've begun the process of becoming someone who leads from within.

This isn't the end of the journey—it's the beginning of a more focused, intentional, and powerfully aligned version of it. So take what you've built here and keep going. The richest things you create—within and around you—start now.

Your Custom Roadmap

Collect your clearest intentions, most powerful affirmations and resources, and next aligned actions—all in one place. Keep it somewhere you'll see often. Update it as you grow.

My Definite Desire

_____

_____

Why This Matters

_____

_____

Action Steps

_____

_____

Personal Affirmations

_____

_____

Master Mind Team

_____

_____

Daily Practice Trackers

	Morning	Evening		Morning	Evening		Morning	Evening
MONDAY	●	●	MONDAY	●	●	MONDAY	●	●
TUESDAY	●	●	TUESDAY	●	●	TUESDAY	●	●
WEDNESDAY	●	●	WEDNESDAY	●	●	WEDNESDAY	●	●
THURSDAY	●	●	THURSDAY	●	●	THURSDAY	●	●
FRIDAY	●	●	FRIDAY	●	●	FRIDAY	●	●
SATURDAY	●	●	SATURDAY	●	●	SATURDAY	●	●
SUNDAY	●	●	SUNDAY	●	●	SUNDAY	●	●

	Morning	Evening		Morning	Evening		Morning	Evening
MONDAY	●	●	MONDAY	●	●	MONDAY	●	●
TUESDAY	●	●	TUESDAY	●	●	TUESDAY	●	●
WEDNESDAY	●	●	WEDNESDAY	●	●	WEDNESDAY	●	●
THURSDAY	●	●	THURSDAY	●	●	THURSDAY	●	●
FRIDAY	●	●	FRIDAY	●	●	FRIDAY	●	●
SATURDAY	●	●	SATURDAY	●	●	SATURDAY	●	●
SUNDAY	●	●	SUNDAY	●	●	SUNDAY	●	●

	Morning	Evening		Morning	Evening		Morning	Evening
MONDAY	●	●	MONDAY	●	●	MONDAY	●	●
TUESDAY	●	●	TUESDAY	●	●	TUESDAY	●	●
WEDNESDAY	●	●	WEDNESDAY	●	●	WEDNESDAY	●	●
THURSDAY	●	●	THURSDAY	●	●	THURSDAY	●	●
FRIDAY	●	●	FRIDAY	●	●	FRIDAY	●	●
SATURDAY	●	●	SATURDAY	●	●	SATURDAY	●	●
SUNDAY	●	●	SUNDAY	●	●	SUNDAY	●	●

	Morning	Evening		Morning	Evening		Morning	Evening
MONDAY	●	●	MONDAY	●	●	MONDAY	●	●
TUESDAY	●	●	TUESDAY	●	●	TUESDAY	●	●
WEDNESDAY	●	●	WEDNESDAY	●	●	WEDNESDAY	●	●
THURSDAY	●	●	THURSDAY	●	●	THURSDAY	●	●
FRIDAY	●	●	FRIDAY	●	●	FRIDAY	●	●
SATURDAY	●	●	SATURDAY	●	●	SATURDAY	●	●
SUNDAY	●	●	SUNDAY	●	●	SUNDAY	●	●